I0492380

Dedication

Dedicated to all who dream, to my mother/editor Barbara, my wonderful family, and my amazing staff.

The information contained in this book does not constitute legal advice and is for information purposes only

CONTENTS

INTRODUCTION

When I launched my career as a lawyer, it wasn't long before I realized that something didn't seem quite right. I had the benefit of being a prosecutor and doing lawyery stuff, like going to court for divorces, shareholder battles and other byzantine legal procedures in a style that dates back to Napoleonic times.

Before law school at Sherbrooke University, I studied Physiology and Management in my first round of Bachelors at McGill University. During that time, I was working part-time at a restaurant for extra cash and even leveraged my student loans to invest in real estate. I started understanding a thing or two about business.

In this day and age, businesses succeed by adapting to consumers' wants, and those that capture market share are able to adapt and innovate faster than their competitors.

But in the legal industry, clients didn't seem to have much influence on how services were being offered.

When I was hired in a small law firm, I noticed there was always tension between client and attorney over billing. Clients were petrified of getting their bill, and for every client that sought out a lawyer, I knew there were countless others who avoided hiring an attorney due to the cost and fear of landing in the proverbial "Shark Tank".

Why weren't law firms adapting to clients and creating new and innovative ways of better serving their clients' legal needs? That feeling of something being not quite right became crystal clear to me.

In 2011, I made it happen. With a 'team' consisting of myself and one intern, I launched Legal Logik with the aim of offering a new, refreshed approach to legal services. By combining technology with a major emphasis on customer service, Legal Logik would put customers needs and results before its own interests.

I focused on building long-term relationships and not on short-term profits, which was often to the firm's detriment. When you let your clients' needs dictate the course of the growth of your business, something amazing happens. It creates the goodwill and credibility to kick-start the organic growth to sustain your vision.

I recognized that the needs of today's entrepreneurs were not best being served by traditional legal services.

We offered free consultations, launched online services like a tech startup, created convenient packages available at flat-fees that people could access even in their pyjamas, and soon…. BOOM…., the firm grew into a full-service, award-winning law firm with nearly 40 staff members and offices in 3 cities.

Legal Logik was and remains committed to making legal services more accessible and affordable to entrepreneurs looking to dedicate their lives to fulfilling their dreams.

We launched our No-Fee Incorporation Service to help startups launch on the right legal footing and have since incorporated thousands of businesses.

Shortly afterwards, we added a full startup package with an incorporation, trademark services and contracts bundled at a price point most law firms charge for an incorporation alone.

We weren't trying to be different and cute for the sake of it, my team and I were different and the market noticed.

Working with thousands of entrepreneurs, startups, and small-medium-sized businesses, I've collected the most common questions, myths, errors and tips and put them into this book.

The book you hold in your hands has a simple but important aim:

> *"Provide an easy-to-understand guide to protect your business, by blowing the lid off the secrets of the pros to keep you on your feet."*

I hope this book helps hone your reflexes for you to make the right decisions for your business, cover your legal blind spots, and maximize your chances of success.

This edition is the first instalment of our journey through the legal maze you will navigate as an entrepreneur.

This edition will focus specifically on legal forms of business, including incorporation, sole proprietorship and partnership.

PART 1: The Ins and Outs of Incorporation

CHAPTER ONE: Choosing the Right Legal Form of Business

"Decide whether to walk alone, ride a tandem bike with your partner or create an empire with you at the throne"

Whon launching your venture, you have the choice of a number of legal forms of business entities available to you. There are advantages and disadvantages to each, and each is tailored to a different set of needs. Choosing the right one for you is the first step to launching any business.

Our governments allow us to decide how we wish to operate our business affairs.

 Decide to be one with a "sole" proprietorship, meaning you are your business and your business is you.

Ride a tandem bike with a partner. By joining activities, you synchronize with the movements of your partner(s).

Create an empire where you declare yourself King (a.k.a. shareholder) with the necessary protection to keep you safe inside a castle. You appoint your guards and advisors and create your own order.

"Doing business without incorporating can feel like bringing a toothpick to a sword fight"

Imagine you've left your job and ploughed your life savings into your new engineering firm, called *Engineerz R us*. You immediately sign a lease and spend tens of thousands of dollars to get your office looking all snazzy. You then hurriedly invest in your branding, hang your sign on the front of the building and get to work calling potential clients. You are pumped and finally living a lifelong dream.

But the honeymoon doesn't last long. The morning after your epic launch party that lasted until the wee hours of the morning, a bailiff rings your doorbell and slaps you with a lawsuit from your former employer, *Engineerz R them*.

Engineerz R them based the lawsuit on the non-compete agreement you previously signed with them, which is still valid for another year. And if that weren't enough, they also claim that you took off with their proprietary files and client lists and are illegally soliciting their clients to directly compete with them. They are seeking an injunction to stop you from operating.

Your dream has turned into a nightmare, and you are now tied up in a court case, fighting tooth and nail to salvage your new business. Unable to pay your bills, you start defaulting on your loans, rent and payroll.

If *Engineerz R us* is a Sole Proprietorship

In this case, as a sole proprietor, any of these creditors will be able to come after your personal assets including any Retirement plans, vehicles, family home and any other assets under you name. This can be a catastrophic moment for an entrepreneur and can seriously jeopardize the family's assets.

If *Engineerz R us* is Incorporated

In this circumstance, the creditors would be limited to pursuing the corporation for repayment. If incorporated, our engineer entrepreneur's personal assets wouldn't have been affected unless he had personally pledged them as a guaranteed.

Now let's take a closer look at the 3 most common forms of business entities.

The Sole Proprietorship

The sole proprietorship is often chosen by small, local businesses and self-employed individuals. Rather than existing as a separate legal entity distinct from the person who creates it, the sole proprietorship is composed of one individual whose personal assets and liabilities are commingled with those of the business.

> *"Having 2 accounts at different banks under your personal name is not a legal protection strategy"*

I consult with too many sole proprietors who are under the misguided impression that they are protected from creditors merely by having two bank accounts at two different institutions; for example, one from which they do their shopping at Costco for their family, and the other where they deposit their business revenues. This is not an appropriate legal strategy because both accounts lead back to the same person!

Entrepreneurs often choose this form of business, as it is the most simple, affordable and easily set up option.

Registration and maintenance costs are low and management and all ongoing administration of a sole proprietorship is simple and straightforward.

Most jurisdictions won't even require you to register as long as you are operating under your personal name. The Government (in all its glory!) can become involved at the moment you choose to operate your business using anything other than your given name, as indicated on your birth certificate. The moment you start operating a business under a different alias is the moment you need to register your business. This is required as well if you need to hire employees, as you'll have to apply for your government numbers.

In another example, other larger businesses with whom you want to transact may require you to register your new business, for tax and/or legal reasons. These established corporations may require you to have tax numbers for their own reporting requirements.

There are a few disadvantages, however.

Since the business and individual are, under the law, considered the same entity, if the business incurs debts that it cannot pay, the individual will be held personally responsible for the repayment. This means that creditors or other third parties can go after the individual's personal assets in seeking repayment if they have a judgment against the business and attack assets such as the family home, vehicle or even savings.

In the event the business cannot pay its debts and declares bankruptcy, this also implies personal bankruptcy for the person behind the business.

Lastly, a sole proprietorship lives on only as long as its owner. It will cease to exist upon the individual's death, declaration of bankruptcy, or the institution of any kind of protective supervision of the business owner (for example, in the event of incapacity). At that time, there may also be devastating tax consequences, in absence of any estate or succession planning by the deceased entrepreneur.

It's not all about the money though. Your accountant, with all his experience, may not suggest incorporation because of the costs, or because you're not generating sufficient revenue yet to justify its creation, so ultimately many new small businesses start out as sole proprietorships.

Your lawyer will tend to see things from a different perspective. Because he is more focused on protecting your assets, he will be more inclined to suggest incorporating, to offset higher risk entrepreneurial ventures.

The Partnership

A partnership is based upon a written or oral agreement (hopefully written!) that governs all aspects of the partnership, including how decisions will be made, which assets (like machinery or patents) each partner will contribute, and the distribution of profits or losses.

In contrast to the sole proprietorship, a partnership exists distinctly from those who create it, and the partners may be responsible for the partnership's obligations.

A partnership can enter into contracts in its own name, acquire credit based on its own pool of assets, institute lawsuits, and also be sued. The "partners", who may be both individuals and/or corporations, do not own the assets of the partnership, but rather own "units", or a percentage of the partnership, as set out by their agreement.

A partnership is often chosen when the parties want the benefit of accessing the joint pool of assets and skill sets contributed proportionally by each party. These pooled assets can be used as collateral to make partnerships more attractive to financial institutions for granting loans and other credit facilities.

A partnership, like a sole proprietorship, also offers benefits such as fairly low registration and maintenance costs. From an income tax perspective, a partnership is not a separate legal person or entity, and each partner is taxed individually on their respective portion of the income/loss of the partnership. Similar to the sole proprietorship, this generally allows partners to deduct losses incurred by the partnership from their own personal revenues, thereby reducing their taxable income.

On one hand, a partnership is known as an "incomplete legal person", as partners often remain personally liable for any debts the partnership incurs. For instance, an action posed (contracted) by one partner may also bind the partnership.

On the other hand, partnerships in Quebec can exist in various forms. For example, partners may choose to adopt a "limited partnership" whereby the "limited" or "special" partners would only be liable for the debt proportionate to their individual contribution to the partnership. For example, a partner owning 40% of the partnership would only be liable for 40% of any incurred debt.

In many cases, parties launch a partnership without a written and signed partnership agreement and then find themselves in a complex legal battle after the fact, trying to sort these issues out.

Although a court may deduce that a partnership was created between parties even in absence of a written agreement, you never want to have a judge substitute their interpretation of your business deal with what you originally intended to achieve as a group.

Partners may differ in opinion, vision, management style and choice of strategy, so it can be difficult to conclude a partnership agreement with the unanimous support from all involved, so make sure to discuss these consideration from outset and put it in writing.

The Corporation

Unlike the sole proprietorship and the partnership, a corporation is a separate legal entity, distinct from its founders, who in turn benefit from limited liability, as their personal assets remain independent from those of the corporation. If a corporation incurs debts or goes bankrupt, creditors cannot pursue the personal assets of the directors or shareholders (unless they've personally guaranteed the debt).

Incorporating brings with it a number of other benefits not offered by the other legal forms of business.

For one, the corporation continues to exist following the death or retirement of any of its founders.

Secondly, corporations have access to a greater variety of financing models, with the ability to issue shares to third party investors, should they qualify, or, if the timing is right, to the public at large.

Thirdly, corporations also benefit from numerous and important tax advantages. Corporate tax rates are generally lower than individual tax rates, therefore tax can be generally deferred if earned through a corporation as long as the "income" is not paid to the shareholder by way of a dividend, for example, and stays or is reinvested in the corporation.

Lastly, if you plan on selling your business, incorporating offers considerable tax exemptions on your taxable capital gains. For instance, selling qualified small business corporation ("QSBC") shares which are generally shares (held for a period of 24 months or more) of a Canadian-controlled private corporation that uses at least 90 percent of its assets in an active business in Canada, could provide the owner a one-time (lifetime) personal capital gains tax exemption of up to $848,252 in 2018.

These benefits make incorporation a very popular option, however there are a some drawbacks.

Establishing a corporation is a more complex procedure, and requires at least some degree of knowledge in corporate law. Founders must first decide whether to incorporate the business under federal laws (the *Canada Business Corporations Act*), or under provincial laws (i.e. Quebec, Ontario, etc.), depending on where the corporation is seeking to set up to do business.

Generally, local businesses will choose to incorporate under the laws of the province in which they operate, whereas businesses with national/international objectives (i.e. transport, telecommunications, etc.) will incorporate under federal law. However, federally incorporated businesses are also required to register with the Provincial Business Registry if they plan on conducting activities in each and every particular province.

At the outset of starting a corporation, you must also:

- Complete the Articles of Incorporation
- Conduct a name search to ensure that the proposed name is not currently registered
- Register the subscribing shareholders
- Elect the directors and officers
- Organize the corporation's minute book (See Chapter 8: Do You Need A Corporate Minute Book?)

Maintaining a corporation also requires additional steps each year. In addition to filing the corporation's tax return, directors and shareholders must file separate tax returns and financial statements. There are also a number of yearly requirements to keep your corporation in good legal standing, which we'll discuss in a later section of this book.

No matter which legal form a business ultimately adopts, those operating in Quebec will also be subject to the *Act Respecting the Legal Publicity of Enterprises* and the *Charter of the French Language*. Both these laws require a business to adopt filing and registration requirements, as well as stringent rules with respect to the language of the business name.

Individuals, partnerships and corporations alike, should consider consulting a legal professional to help them in making the right choice for their particular needs in order to get their new businesses off to the right start.

NOTES:

CHAPTER TWO: 8 Advantages of Incorporation

> *"An incorporation is the canvas*
> *for your business story"*

SUMMARY

1. Business Longevity

2. Limited Liability

3. Lower Tax Rate

4. Tax Deferral

5. Offset Losses

6. Payout Options

7. Securing Funding

8. Tax Exemptions When Selling

THE TOP 8 ADVANTAGES OF INCORPORATION

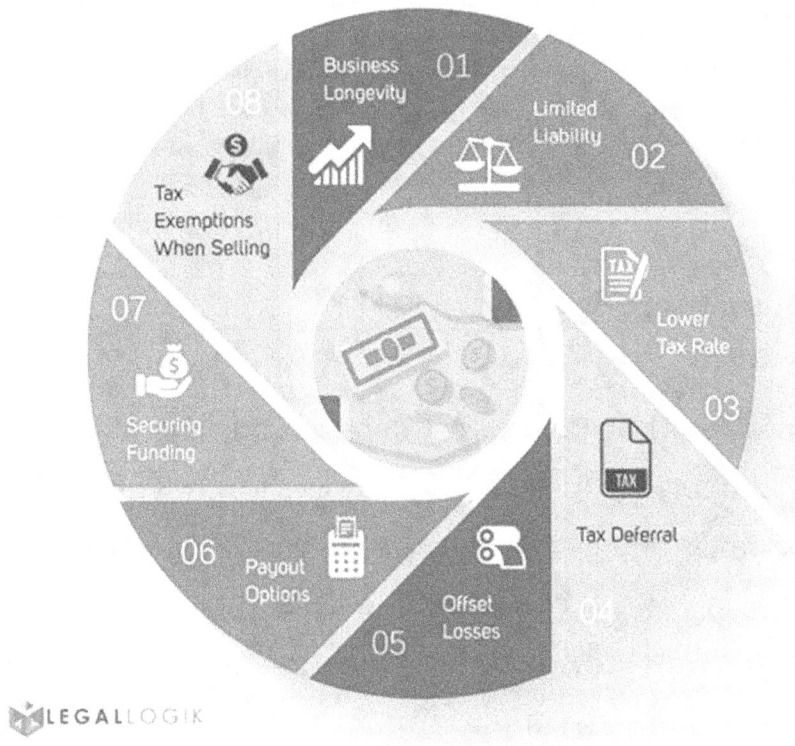

Incorporation is the most popular business entity, because of the advantages it offers to help businesses cover their legal bases, cut their taxes and build wealth.

Let's delve into these benefits in more depth so you can determine which of them is most important for your business.

1. Business Longevity

Our society has conceived unbelievably creative ways of introducing unique concepts to advance our economies and better organize capital, risk and reward.

Governments have made it possible for risk takers in business to create joint stock companies that allow them to separate themselves from the business itself and permit that entity to exist indefinitely. As long as its legal and tax obligations are fulfilled, it is properly funded, and the shareholders continue to believe in its mission, the corporation can continue to exist.

> **"Incorporating allows its founders to leave behind a legacy that transcends generations"**

Let's take the Hudson's Bay Company of Canada, one of the oldest corporations in existence in the Great White North, as an example. The Bay was created in 1670 by two French traders who left Europe for the New World, in search of creating a fur trading post along the northern and western coasts of Lake Superior.

The traders, Pierre-Esprot Radisson and Médard de Chouar, first approached the French government, hoping to receive funding for their expeditions. They needed to kick-start their business, but their attempts were quickly rebuffed. After serving time in prison for allegedly trading fur without a license, they ultimately caught their break after a serendipitous encounter with a couple of English Bostonians who introduced them to Prince Rupert of England. The Prince supported their idea and proceeded to fund their plan.

Fast track 300 years later, and the Hudson Bay Corporation, now known as "The Bay," still exists, having successfully redefined itself repeatedly over the centuries, weathering countless recessions and ever-changing retail trends.

This is what is meant when discussing longevity. Those two French founders of Hudson's Bay could never have envisioned the depth and scope of the reality of their entrepreneurial dreams, let alone imagine that it would continue to impact our lives today.

When you incorporate your business, you create a distinct legal entity separate from yourself. This is not the case with any other legal form of business. In a sole proprietorship, for example, your business will cease to exist upon your death.

As a separate legal entity, a corporation is granted the possibility of longevity. You can put a succession plan in place and pass the business to your future heirs, or sell it altogether. This means the corporation you create can live on beyond your own lifetime, leaving a legacy over generations.

Think of some of the world's most successful companies. You'd see that every single one was a legal entity separate from its founder, to allow for the potential of growth beyond the founder's lifetime. Incorporation, therefore, becomes an important vehicle to consider on the path to creating tradition and legacy.

2. Limited Liability

Entrepreneurs can limit their liability, as we learned above in the *Engineerz R us* case.

There is a compelling case to be made about limited liability and its effects, without which the risks and exposure of your new venture may jeopardize the assets you worked so hard to accumulate during your lifetime.

Since you create a separate legal entity from yourself when you incorporate your business, you benefit from what is called limited liability. What this means is that, as a director or shareholder of the corporation, in most circumstances, you cannot be held personally responsible for the corporation's debts or obligations.

If the corporation is sued or goes bankrupt, the business's assets will be at stake, but not your personal assets, such as savings, a home or a vehicle. You might lose your investment in the corporation, but you won't be responsible for any other amounts the corporation owes.

Remember, however, that limited liability does not mean unlimited liability, as there are certain situations when directors of a corporation can be held liable, as in the instance of unpaid wages.

3. Lower Tax Rate

When you go into business, you automatically partner with the government, who is eager to take their share of every hard earned dollar that you generate, whether you like it or not.

But what if there was a way to reduce the amount of the government's share on every dollar brought in by a business owner? Reduce their share from every chocolate bar you sell, from every real estate deal you close, from every massage you give, or license to every product you grant?

As discussed above, when you earn revenue through a non-incorporated business, such as a sole proprietorship, you will be taxed at a higher tax rate than the rates generally applicable to corporations. This is one reason why incorporation is a central element of every business model.

The corporation's lower tax rates may also allow for the deferral of the payment of taxes to a later date, at which time you can pay the earned revenue out as dividends and/or salary.

Note that this lower tax rate is for active business income and may not apply to passive income such as rental income and capital gains, which is why accountants usually don't recommend incorporating for small real estate ventures.

4. Tax Deferral

Savvy entrepreneurs understand that the value of their money today is higher than its future value.

If that's the accepted truism, why pay taxes now when you can pay it at a later time and put your money to work for you today? It may be cliché, but the adage "*Money Never Sleeps*" is the motto of many successful people who have accumulated fortunes.

With a little financial planning and some good tax advice, you can keep more money in your bank account today. Although you can't avoid paying taxes indefinitely, you may be able to delay payment at a later time when you may not necessarily need as much cash flow as today to invest in your venture.

As the owner of a non-incorporated sole proprietorship, you are generally taxed at the highest rates on revenues earned under your personal name. When you incorporate, however, you are generally only taxed personally on the money you take out of the corporation: for example, in the form of a salary or dividends.

Tax deferral is a strategy by which you delay paying taxes to some future date. While the net taxes paid should end up being the same, there may be opportunities to benefit from a reduced tax rate in the future, and also increase your business cash flow until then.

> *"Incorporation is to business what the swiss army knife is to MacGyver"*

5. Offset Losses

It takes years of discipline, recovering from mistakes, and many sleepless nights to get to a point where your business is running on cruise control.

Entrepreneurship is like running a marathon: it takes a lot of training and practice until you can achieve profitability and, unless you are the exceptional exception, you are unlikely to be profitable or cash flow positive for the first few years of your business operations. This creates another advantage if you are incorporated.

A business that is incorporated has the added benefit of being able to use losses that have been accumulated in previous years with potential taxes to be paid on future revenue.

This means that you can use your losses during the harder days of business development to your corporation's benefit, by paying less taxes to the government on your future revenue.

If you put your nose to the grindstone, and surround yourself with the right complementary personnel... you too can experience this euphoric tax phenomenon!

No matter what legal form of business you choose, you won't be taxed if the business incurs losses. Each legal form of business deals with losses differently, however you can generally offset future income with these losses.

6. Payout Options

Incorporating offers you additional financial options not available to other forms of business entities. When you incorporate, you can choose how to remunerate shareholders and directors, either with a salary or through dividends which can result in significant tax advantages.

If you hire family members, the corporation could deduct their salaries as an expense. You can also make family members or associates shareholders and pay them - as well as yourself - through dividends, which are often taxed at a reduced rate.

To determine the best payout options for your corporation, speak to an accountant or fiscalist.

7. Securing Funding

Our client *John T. Startup* was grinding every night in his mother's basement trying to create a new application. It allowed users on social media platforms to identify who was peeking at each other's profiles, in the hope of generating matches for business, love or leisure, depending on the user's interests.

The technology behind it was innovative, and he had spent all of his *Bar Mitzvah* money creating the platform, with the goal of exiting with a buyout offer from one of the giant social media companies.

He worked tirelessly every day into the wee hours of the morning, and eventually, after applying for multiple loans and bursaries, and harassing the developers and managers of social media platforms, the call that *John T. Startup* prayed for was answered.

After a few telephone conversations, the acquisition director of a large social media group sent him a term sheet with the goal of making a significant investment in his business.

The problem was that *John T. Startup* was completely disorganized. He had unfavourable agreements with different agencies in India and Bulgaria that helped him develop aspects of the project, and he had failed to protect his intellectual property.

Most alarmingly to the investor was that John T. neglected to take the time to incorporate and commingled all of his personal affairs with that of the business.

During any transaction, the due diligence period allows the potential investor to take a peek inside the business to make sure all is in order before concluding the deal.

This period turned into a nightmare and John T.'s lack of preparedness and foresight prior to soliciting investment dollars raised red flags that proved difficult to overcome. The potential investor lost confidence in *John T. Startup* and the deal died.

If you're looking for funding, incorporation is usually a prerequisite. Lenders and investors want to know you've ensured your corporation's longevity and basic protection through this limited liability vehicle.

Of course, you'll still have to pitch your business model, provide financials and perhaps even offer collateral, but incorporating your business may give you the edge that you need.

8. Tax Exemptions When Selling

Planning to sell the shares of your business? Make sure it's incorporated, as you can benefit from attractive tax exemptions on your capital gains.

As discussed above, selling your Qualified Small Business Corporation (QSBC) shares in a Canadian-controlled private corporation that uses at least 90% of its assets to do business in Canada could make you eligible to claim a one-time personal capital-gains tax exemption of $848,252 in 2018.

Notes:

CHAPTER THREE: Limited Liability Demystified: The Benefits and Limitations of Incorporation

"Incorporating will protect the business owner like a bullet-proof vest, but negligence, like a missile, will go right through"

One of the benefits of incorporation is limited liability for shareholders. Since you're creating a separate legal entity, as a shareholder, in most circumstances, you can't be held personally responsible for the corporation's debts or obligations.

If the corporation is sued or goes bankrupt, the business's assets will be at stake, but not your personal assets such as savings, a home or a vehicle. You might lose your investment in the corporation, but you won't be responsible for any other amounts the corporation owes.

But limited liability does not mean unlimited liability. In some cases, directors can be held personally liable.

1. Negligence

If you're aware of a problem, fail to address it, and thereafter cause injury or damages to someone, you can be held liable. A court of law may hold you responsible for paying damages, and sometimes even incur the other party's legal costs.

Kelly Kale left her boring office job a few years back to start an organic juice business downtown. The business plan was ready, the incorporation was freshly registered under *Kelly Kale Inc.* and the lease was negotiated.

The second Kelly opened her doors the response was amazing: bloggers blogged, instagrammers loved the vivid colours and decor and she tripled the expected revenue month-over-month consistently for years.

However, one incident would forever change the course of her beloved juice shop.

Several months earlier, Kelly received an email from her main supplier out of California, advising her that the previous three shipments of kale to her shop were recalled across the country because of a potential E. Coli contamination. Kelly thanked the representative in writing.

Despite knowing about the recalled kale, Kelly ignored the warnings from her supplier and national news reports regarding the four people that died from consuming kale and who's autopsy reports corroborated traces of E. Coli from kale consumption.

Despite what she knew, Kelly continued to use the recalled kale in her juice.

Imagine her shock when she received a lawyer's letter advising her that a customer of her shop was in critical condition at the hospital with potential E. Coli poisoning after consuming her popular kale smoothie. The victim's family held *Kelly Kale Inc.* and Kelly personally liable for the poisoning. Kelly's customer died days later in the hospital.

The victim's family sued, and it was revealed that Kelly ignored warnings from her supplier and failed to take the necessary and reasonable precautions to rid her kitchen of the recalled kale.

The judge sided with the victim's family and declared both *Kelly Kale Inc.* and Kelly personally negligent for failing to act diligently as an administrator of the corporation and ordered them to pay an amount of twenty million dollars in compensation and punitive damages.

Both *Kelly Kale Inc.* and Kelly personally went bankrupt months later.

2. Fraud

If you make untrue or exaggerated claims about a product, solicit consumers with fraudulent offers, or provide incorrect or misleading information to shareholders or regulators, you can be charged with fraud.

Fraud is a criminal offence, and an individual found guilty may face prison time and be personally liable for damages in a separate civil suit.

Kelly Kale may be charged with criminal negligence in the E. Coli debacle.

3. Personal Guarantee of a Contract

If, as a shareholder, you personally guaranteed a corporation's debts, the rules of limited liability does not apply. In the event that the Corporation cannot pay its debts, you can be held personally liable for make those payments.

4. Professional Malpractice

If you're a professional, such as a doctor, lawyer or accountant, incorporating will not limit your professional liability for negligence or professional misconduct.

If you make a mistake, cause personal injury to a client, or fail to deliver services as expected, you can be held personally liable. This is why, as a professional, even when incorporated, your professional order requires that you have and maintain professional liability insurance.

Even though as a professional you may benefit from professional liability insurance, an incorporation can personally protect you from business activities unrelated to your core activities as a professional. This is the case if your office lease, contractors you deal with, etc., all deal exclusively with your professional corporation.

Take the example of the professional who is no longer able to practice due to a debilitating medical condition. In the event he can no longer operate his practice and is in default with respect to his rent and other bills, his suppliers and creditors will only be able to come after the professional corporation. Although his professional liability insurance will not cover these instances, the creditors will not be able to hold him personally liable without a personal guarantee.

That being said, it is often recommended for professionals to create a management or administrative corporation separate from their core professional activities. Take the example of a medical clinic, where a group of doctors not only practice medicine but run an office that has administrative staff, business dealings and other considerations. In this case, you can expect the founding doctors to also be shareholders of a nonprofessional corporation as a front through which all the nurses, administrative personnel and doctors' billings are administered.

5. Actions that "Pierce the Veil" of the Corporation

A corporation is considered a separate legal entity from its shareholders. The protection offered by limited liability is often blurred when shareholders commingle their personal affairs with those of the corporation they control.

Several specific actions can "pierce the corporate veil", leaving the shareholders behind the protective veil exposed to personal liability.

Mixing business and personal funds or using business assets for personal needs are the most common ways to trigger this.

Personal and business funds should be kept separate and financial transactions properly documented. If a shareholder takes money from the corporation, this should be properly recorded as a loan, dividend or otherwise in the corporation's financial statements and recorded in its minute book.

Corporate Directors: What You're Liable For

The rules of liability are different for the directors and officers that manage the day to day operations of a corporation. As in the above example, If a shareholder has another role, such as director, in certain cases he or she may be liable for the obligations and proper functioning of the corporation.

1. Duty of Care

The *Canada Business Corporations Act* (CBCA) stipulates that directors and officers of a corporation have a duty of care towards the corporation. What this means is that they must exercise a reasonable level of care and diligence during their administration of the corporation and must act honestly, in good faith, and in the best interests of the corporation.

2. Remain Informed

The directors and officers of a corporation cannot avoid personal liability by pleading ignorance on the grounds that they did not know what the corporation was doing.

The CBCA states that each director is obligated to be informed as to what activities the corporation is undertaking, ensure that they are legal, and in the best interests of the corporation.

3. Prevent Conflicts of Interest

The CBCA obligates directors and officers of a corporation to disclose, in writing, any conflicts of interest that may exist between their personal interests and those of the corporation. If this isn't done, the court can intervene to sanction this behaviour.

The powers of the court are quite extensive in these types of cases. A court can order the return of the corporation's property held by the director, or even terminate the contract the director signed if he acted beyond his authority and/or if it is proven to be contrary to the corporation's best interests.

As an example, if a director buys a yacht or a jet on behalf of the corporation beyond his authority and/or without it having the financial capacity to afford it, the court can (upon petition from an interested person) cancel the transaction, return the money spent back to the corporation and/or intervene to reestablish order.

4. Specific Liabilities

There are exceptional circumstances in which directors of a corporation may be held liable for particular debts.

In some cases, directors may be held liable for up to six months worth of unpaid salary and government benefits to employees of the corporation and government tax obligations.

Protecting Yourself from the Limits of Limited Liability

There are hacks for you to use to protect yourself from being exposed behind by the veil of limited liability.

1. Get Insured

John T. Board is a high profile investor and business personality in the city, and is frequently asked to join the Board of Directors of both private and nonprofit corporations.

John has been around the block enough times to know that limited liability does not mean unlimited liability and has seen firsthand how a good E&O (Errors and Omission) insurance policy can protect the corporation and its directors in sticky situations.

John was asked to join the Board of a local nonprofit corporation that generates awareness for mental illness, a cause dear to his heart, since members of his family have been affected. He gladly accepts the role and challenge to turn things around for the struggling organization.

John joins the Board and begins attending the annual assemblies and special meetings to put in place new measures and protocols. While digging into the past, John realizes that the organization had not been making its employees sign contracts and the terms of employment were vague.

John works tirelessly with the organization's lawyers to put in place the proper contracts and HR protocols but it's too late for certain employees that have loyally served the organization for years.

During a recent round of job cuts, John led the organization in cutting 30% of the its administrative workforce in an effort to streamline operations.

One such packaged employee immediately files a complaint with the Labour Board against the organization, as well as all directors personally, including John T. Board.

The employee is citing unjust dismissal and that unpaid vacation pay was due going back 18 months.

John alerts the organization's insurance of the recent complaint, who immediately take over the case in their stead. After a year-long legal battle the organization was not held liable for any damages or unpaid vacation as claimed by the employee.

The story of John T. Board could have ended up very differently had there not been a proper insurance policy in place. Not only would he and the organization have had to assume legal fees, but in the event the directors were deemed liable for any part of the employee's claim, John T. could have been ordered to pay the same amounts personally. This is a dangerous scenario, especially since he was volunteering his time to the organization.

Various types of insurance are available to protect both directors and officers against liabilities that can be incurred while performing their duties. The right insurance policy may pay your legal fees in the case of a lawsuit and even cover the cost of damages should you lose.

Your insurer may also require that certain policies and practices be implemented in your corporation to prevent negligence, such as employee manuals and other policies that an HR consultant can help you put in place.

2. Sign a Shareholders' Agreement

A professionally drafted shareholders' agreement can transfer some or all of a director's responsibilities and powers to shareholders.

In this case, since duties and responsibilities have been transferred away from the director, that director may not be held responsible for not performing the duty in question.

We'll go deeper on considerations when drafting a shareholder's agreement in the last chapter (see Chapter 10: Do You Need A Shareholders' Agreement?).

3. HR [Human Resources] Best Practices

Employment-related matters are a minefield of potential

liability, for both your corporation and yourself, so it's crucial for any organization to ensure its HR practices are protecting it rather than allowing vague relationships to subsist and bog down the business.

A director has the legal (fiduciary) responsibility towards the employees of a corporation. If these responsibilities are not met, the director may be held personally liable, as in the case of failing to adequately supervise employees or monitor the conduct of those employees in their work for the corporation. For example, as an employer, you are obligated by law to provide a work environment free of harassment or discrimination.

Failure to effectively do so leaves you open to legal claims, both against yourself and your corporation. How can you ensure you live up to these responsibilities? You must develop internal policies for complying with the laws and issues related to harassment and discrimination, should they arise.

Investing the time and effort up front can help reduce the risk of corporate liability and help keep your business from becoming entangled in expensive, lengthy, and reputation-damaging   litigation.

At a glance, it might seem simple – just comply with your legal duties as a director or officer of a corporation. The problem is that there is a multitude of laws governing the actions of directors and officers in various situations.

To protect yourself, the best offense will always be a good defense. A legal advisor can help you identify risks associated with your business and industry, anticipate problems or situations that may engage your liability, and develop customized risk management strategies.

Incorporating offers the benefit of limited liability, which is just that: limited. Incorporation is just one piece of the legal pie to help protect your assets and build a business on a solid legal foundation.

Notes:

CHAPTER FOUR: Should You Incorporate Your Business?

These 6 Questions Will Help You Decide

SUMMARY

1. Do you want to protect your assets?

2. Will your business generate substantial profit?

3. How fast will your business generate a profit?

4. Do you want to raise capital?

5. Do you plan to sell your business?

6. Does your business involve considerable risk?

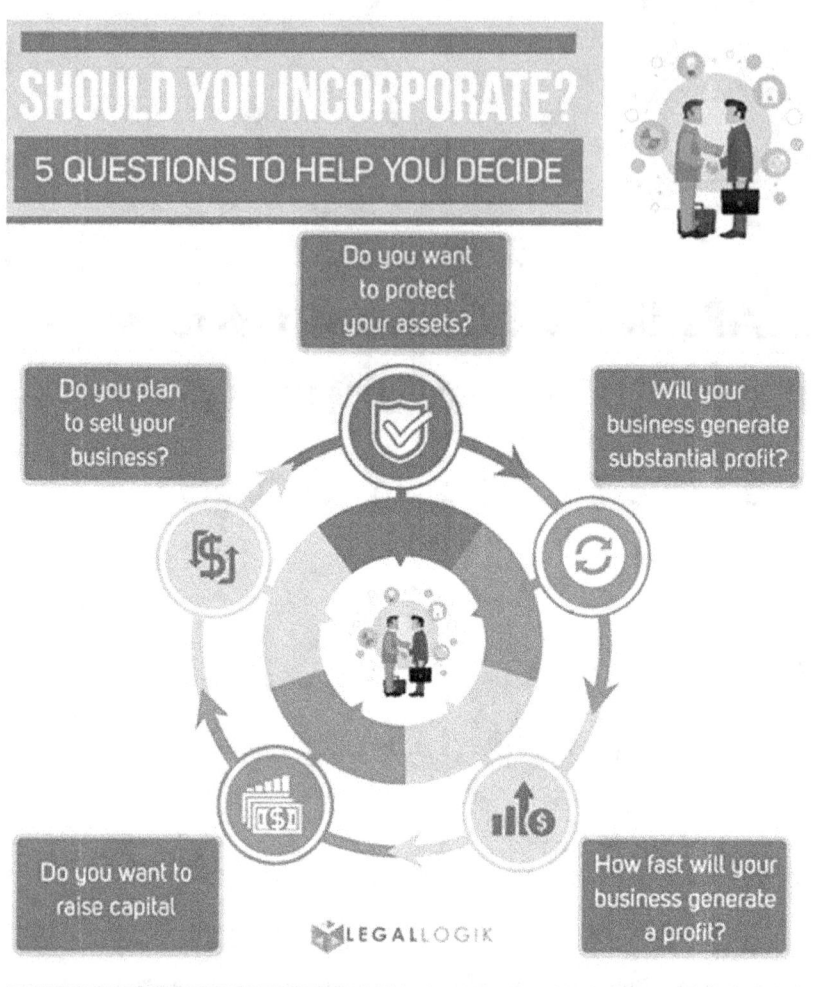

© Legal Logik, used under license

When starting a corporation, there's a variety of different legal forms of business to choose from. Each one has specific advantages, but if you're aiming for growth, only incorporation gives you a lineup of benefits that will help you protect your assets and set a foundation for the growth of your business.

So should you incorporate? These 5 questions will help you decide.

1. Do you want to protect your assets?

As a sole proprietor, you're liable for any debts your business incurs. If you fail to pay a supplier, that supplier can come after your home, car and personal savings. The same is true for most other forms of business. If you've formed a general partnership, or are part of a joint venture, you and the other partners may be responsible for certain obligations of the business.

Incorporating offers you limited liability. This means that in the event of a lawsuit or bankruptcy, you won't be held personally responsible. You might lose your initial investment, but you won't lose your home, car, or other personal assets that are not guaranteeing the business debts. No other form of business offers this level of protection.

2. Will your business generate substantial profit?

Accountants often use a shortcut to help you decide whether you should be incorporating: will you earn more revenue than you'll need to draw from the business in order to live on? If so, incorporating may reduce the amount of tax you could be paying, especially when you consider the excess cash remaining in the corporation.

When you incorporate, you are generally taxed at a lower rate compared with revenue earned as a sole proprietorship.

There are some exceptions however. When you generate passive income, such as from real estate rental income, you may be taxed at the highest personal rate. In these cases, incorporating may not offer any tax advantages.

3. How fast will your business generate a profit?

When starting a business, it might take a few years to recuperate your initial investment. As a sole proprietor, the losses you incur in the first few years of operation may, with certain conditions, be deducted against other types of income you earn, such as employment or investment income.

On the other hand, if you're incorporated but are not generating sufficient revenue, losses may be applied against the corporation's future revenue to reduce the tax implications at that time.

For example, capital losses can generally only offset capital gains. If you don't expect to earn a profit in your early years and you're in a low-risk business, it might make sense to put off incorporating until you grow, unless you believe that other, less tax-driven considerations, justify putting it in place, such as corporate structure, personal liability or the ability to attract   investors.

4. Do you want to raise capital?

If you want to raise money to grow your business, incorporation is the way to go. Most entrepreneurs bootstrap their operations or try to get a business loan. Corporations do facilitate capital raises in the following ways. First, incorporations tend to be more attractive to investors due to the added security (limited liability). Second, as a separate legal entity, you can issue shares to raise immediate capital, and you have flexibility in defining what kind of shares to offer investors.

For example, you can maintain control of your corporation by issuing shares that reward investors with dividends without granting them voting rights.

5. Do you plan to sell your business?

If you're planning to build a business with the aim of selling it, you may want to incorporate. When you sell any business, you're taxed on the capital you make on the sale of your shares. Selling your shares in a corporation offers attractive tax advantages. You could potentially claim a onetime capital gains tax exemption on the sale of a Canadian-controlled private corporation that uses at least 90% of its assets to do business in Canada.

Incorporating involves upfront costs, adds extra paperwork to your to-do list each year, and costs a bit more to maintain. Should you incorporate? If the benefits to your business outweigh those costs, go for it!

6. Does your business involve considerable risk?

Often, entrepreneurs incorporate to take advantage of the tax benefits and to protect their assets through the power of limited liability afforded by the corporate structure. Some ventures and initiatives favour incorporation even if they're not earning enough revenue to benefit from the tax advantages.

If your business or industry involves considerable risk, incorporating may help protect you. If a lawsuit is ever filed against the corporation, you and the other directors/shareholders may not be held responsible for the debts the corporation is condemned to pay by a court of law (unless they've personally guaranteed).

If you are operating a business in any of the following industries, for example, it's a good idea to consider incorporating from the start:

- Serving or selling alcohol (Such as a convenient store, bar, restaurant or entertainment venue)
- Serving, manufacturing or packaging food products
- Using, manufacturing or transporting hazardous materials
- Caring for animals (such as a pet grooming centre)
- Operating a motor vehicle as part of a commercial venture
- Storing or repairing valuables
- Repairing buildings or vehicles

Incorporation for Professionals and Malpractice

Even though as a professional you may benefit from professional liability insurance, the incorporation can still protect you from business activities unrelated to your core activities as a professional. This can be with respect to an office lease entered into with your professional corporation, contractors you deal with, office supplies, etc.

Take the example of the professional who is no longer able to practice due to a debilitating medical condition. In the event he can no longer operate his practice and cannot pay his rent and other obligations, his suppliers and creditors will only be able to come after his professional corporation. Although his professional insurance will not cover these instances, they will not be able to hold him personally liable unless he offered personally guarantees from the beginning.

Notes:

CHAPTER FIVE: Should You Incorporate Provincially or Federally?

4 Questions to Help You Decide

SUMMARY

1. Where will you operate?

2. Do you want added protection for your name?

3. Do you need to cut down on costs?

4. Are the members of your Board of Directors Canadian residents?

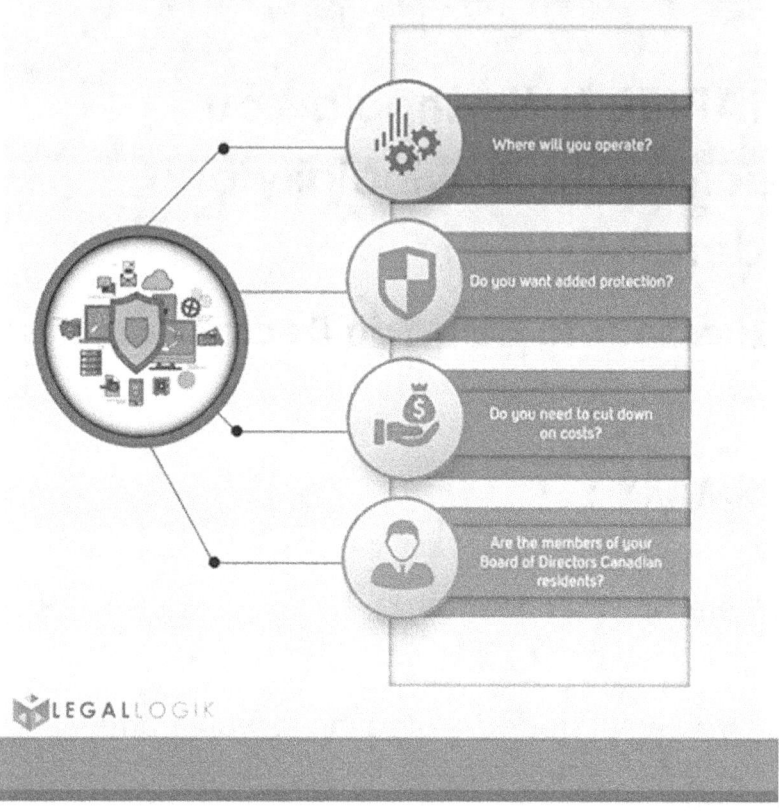

© Legal Logik, used under license

"It's like deciding between Coca-Cola or Pepsi"

When it comes time to incorporate, you've got a decision to make. Should you incorporate provincially or federally? Both offer the same basic advantages and both let you do business anywhere in the world.

I often make the analogy to Coca-Cola and Pepsi, because both offer the same thirst quenching benefits, have the same caloric profile, are the same size, but they taste different. Sometimes you only have one choice, for instance at a restaurant chain that has an exclusivity with one of the brands.

Well, it's the same thing for your incorporation. Both provincial and federal versions are fighting for market share just like the drinks, and some industries even have an exclusivity with a certain jurisdiction, as we'll discuss below.

So how do you pick? Let's take the taste test and consider 4 questions to ask to help you decide which is best for your business.

1. **Where will you operate?**

If you plan to operate in Quebec only, you can incorporate under a provincial charter. If you'll be operating in more than one province, it might be better to incorporate federally. That will make it easier to begin doing business in any of the provinces, and better protects your name nationally.

Franchisees of fast food chains, for example, and other licensed concepts, most commonly open numbered corporations to operate their businesses.

In Quebec it is customary to create a corporation for a new franchise under the numeric designation 1234-5678 Quebec Inc. and subsequently registering the franchisor's trademarked name (i.e. "Bill's Burgers") as a d.b.a. (Doing Business As) name. Similarly, a Canadian corporation can be created to operate Bill's Burgers.

Franchise agreements grant permission to the franchisee to use the renowned trade name, which is tied to a territory within the province in which they operate. Due to the localized restrictions that franchisees must obey, they will typically adopt a provincial charter.

If you incorporate in Quebec and later decide to move your head office, you'll need to file a Certificate of Continuance to change your corporation's charter from provincial to federal. That takes additional time, effort and money to file the certificate – plus applicable professional fees, so it's best to be clear from the outset whether you expect to stay close to home or expand and move your operations in the near future.

2. Do you want added protection for your name?

Incorporating federally gives you added protection across the country or, as Corporations Canada declares: "a status second only to trademark protection".

Before Corporations Canada grants you the right to use a particular corporate name, you must perform what's called a NUANS name search. This verifies the uniqueness of your name within the federal government's corporate name database. If nothing similar exists, your proposed legal name may be published nationally.

If you're aiming for major growth and planning to invest

in your brand nationally, federal incorporation is best. If you incorporate provincially and later decide to expand, the name you incorporated at the beginning might since have been taken by someone else in another Canadian province. You'll need to pick a different name for your business in those provinces, which could hurt your efforts to build your brand.

Although trademarking your brand may neutralize these risks by protecting your business name across the country, you should consult with a trademark agent before making a decision.

3. Do you want to cut down on costs?

Incorporating in Quebec under a provincial charter is a bit easier on the wallet. If you don't need the characteristics of a federal incorporation, you can cut down on costs by registering provincially.

When you incorporate federally, you have to pay the required federal incorporation fees in addition to the provincial fees, both in the province where the head office is located, as well as in each province where you operate.

4. Are the members of your Board of Directors Canadian residents?

Canadian corporate law stipulates that at least one quarter of the Board of Directors of a federal corporation must be Canadian residents. There are no such residency requirements for its Quebec counterpart.

The Dubai-based corporation, *Habibi Exports*, reached out to Legal Logik to open a Canadian division to distribute products that were being imported from Dubai.

Habibi was adamant on opening a Canadian corporation citing the requirements of their investors, under the name *Habibi Imports Canada Inc.*

The problem was that I could not recommend that they open a federal corporation since all of the proposed directors of the new Canadian division resided in Dubai and would travel to Canada intermittently to conduct the affairs of *Habibi Imports Canada Inc.*

So, in this case, the solution was to set them up with a Quebec corporation and list all of the foreign directors and shareholders on the government records. We advised them that in the event they have local management and/or people who take up positions on the board, that we could then convert their existence under a federal charter (a.k.a. by way of a Certificate of Continuance).

Three successful years had passed for *Habibi Imports Canada Inc.*, and they had raised significant capital in Canada. Canadian investors and directors would embark into the Quebec-incorporated affiliate of the Dubai Corporation, and we received instructions to update their charter from a Quebec to a Canadian corporation. This was now possible, given that they now had one out of three members of the board who were Canadian residents.

Whereas there are residency requirements for directors, as we've seen in the case of *Habibi Imports Canada Inc.*, there are no such requirements for shareholders, who can be located locally or internationally.

Notes:

PART 2: Getting it Done

CHAPTER SIX: The Top 6 Incorporation Mistakes and How to Avoid Them

SUMMARY

1. Incorporating under the wrong jurisdiction

2. Describing your corporation incorrectly

3. Not giving your corporation a name

4. Skipping the shareholders agreement

5. Believing that limited liability means unlimited liability

6. Neglecting your corporate records

Incorporating? It might seem simple, but it's a process filled with legal intricacies that you'll need to get right if you want to set a solid legal foundation for business growth.

While it is something you can do on your own, there are a number of common errors people make when taking the do-it-yourself approach, and usually they don't find out until it's too late. The problem can be fixed of course, but not without time, effort and money.

Here are the 6 most common mistakes to avoid to properly incorporate.

1. Incorporating under the wrong jurisdiction

In Canada, you have the choice to incorporate provincially or federally. Which you choose may impact the future of the corporation. Incorporating provincially will cost you less, but if you later decide you want to expand and move your head office beyond the borders of your province, you'll need to file a Certificate of Continuation to change your corporation's jurisdiction from a provincial to a federal charter. By then, someone else might own the rights to your business name in other provinces, unless you've trademarked your brand.

2. Describing your corporation incorrectly

When you incorporate, you have to decide on how your business will be structured. The articles of incorporation clarify what kind of shares the corporation will offer, the voting rights of shareholders, and whether they are entitled to dividends, amongst other things.

Unless you properly describe the share capital and other aspects of the corporation from the start, you will have to perform various modifications, which takes time and often incurs additional fees. The best thing is to leave yourself as much flexibility as possible for growth.

When you incorporate, make sure to create a large range of share classes to offer more options for potential shareholders, providing more options during tax or fiscal planning. Similarly, in anticipation of future growth, you'll want to provide for an unlimited authorized share capital and allow for a wide range of directors. That way, you'll be able to make more decisions regarding your corporate structure without spending money amending your articles as you grow.

3. Not giving your corporation a name

You might be ready to incorporate, but not sure what to name your business. No problem! If you incorporate without a name, the corporation will be given a number that serves as your corporation's legal identifier. You can still use a trade name, but any official business you conduct, such as signing cheques or contracts, will need to be done under your corporation's legal identifier.

A corporate name, however, can be a valuable asset, helping you build your business and your brand. Having an approved federal corporate name provides you with an added degree of protection, granting you the common law rights to that name across Canada, in virtue of its publication in the federal corporate name database (NUANS).

If you want to expand your operations to other provinces, you will be able to operate under that name throughout the country, provided that there is no conflict with any similar name in any other province. If you opted for a numbered corporation when you incorporated and later want to update your legal name, it will cost you.

4. Skipping the shareholders agreement

When launching a business, co-founders can set their sights on growth, leaving formalities like a shareholders agreement on the backburner. Unless you take the time to get it done at the beginning, it might simply be forgotten, and that could be a costly mistake.

No one knows what the future holds, but there are plenty of unplanned events that can occur and negatively impact your corporation. What happens if a shareholder wants to exit the corporation, goes bankrupt, commits fraud, or passes away? The law is silent on these matters and many more, and if they do happen, you'll be left in a legal grey zone, and getting such matters resolved often requires lengthy legal proceedings.

A well-drafted shareholder agreement is the best way to avoid future headaches. It helps protect you against the consequences of unplanned events and their impact on shareholders and the corporation, by setting down in writing what actions will be taken in varying circumstances.

When unexpected events occur, many entrepreneurs have been saved by the terms of the shareholders agreement they made sure to sign at the outset (See Chapter 10: Do You Need A Shareholders Agreement?).

5. Believing that limited liability means unlimited liability

Limited liability is one of the core advantages of incorporating. But while incorporating your business can shield you from personal liability in many cases, there are situations in which you may be held personally responsible for your actions, or those of your staff. If you don't act in the corporation's best interests, commit fraud or are negligent as a director or shareholder, you can be held liable. You can also be held responsible in specific circumstances, such as for unpaid salary or for issuing shares at a price less than the fair market value.

6. Neglecting your corporate records

Each year you must produce an annual declaration for your corporation. At the federal level, if you don't produce your annual declaration for two consecutive years, Corporations Canada will dissolve the corporation. Reactivating your corporation once it has been dissolved will set you back $200 just in costs to Corporations Canada.

In Quebec, if your annual declaration is not filed for two years in a row, the Enterprise Register may remove your business from the database. If you're registered federally, remember you must file both at the federal level and at the provincial level at the provinces where your business operates.

When you incorporate, don't take any chances that might cost you valuable time, energy and money down the road. Make sure to avoid these errors and get some advice from a lawyer. You'll be glad you did!

Notes:

CHAPTER SEVEN: Incorporating: Do You Need A Lawyers' Help?

> *"Consider your lawyer as a coach who ensures you don't fall off the legal sidelines"*

Technology and the Internet have transformed the legal industry, and now it's easier than ever to take the DIY route for important legal steps like incorporation. And this is what many entrepreneurs do to keep their startup costs down.

But should you?

As an attorney, I might be a bit biased, but as an entrepreneur, I look at the question with solid business sense. Let me tell you what I mean.

I once worked with a corporation that had a fantastic

and fast-growing business. Much to their excitement, they received an attractive offer from an investor. They were poised to get an injection of cash and take things to the next level, but soon realized there was a problem.

When they incorporated, they did not provide the proper share description. In other words, the entrepreneurs did not want to give the investor the only available share class (Class A shares with voting rights). The problem was that the investor expected to receive that class of shares since that was the only share class authorized by the corporation from the beginning. The result was delays from the investor, and he eventually pulled out, telling the directors of the corporation that they were unorganized.

Providing the proper share description is one of the technical intricacies of incorporating. It's very easy to overlook, but needs to be done right.

I often joke that many of my best clients are businesses who incorporated on their own and made a few mistakes, meaning that the corporation wasn't set up in a way that allowed them to do what they needed during the crucial years of business growth. My team and I are hired to get the corporation back on track, reorganizing the corporate structure, so that the options the directors and shareholders want are available to them.

We'll do this, but we much prefer saving a new corporation from troubles like this right from the start. In this case, if they had invested a little more in setting things up right at the beginning, it would have saved them time and money down the road. Just a short consultation could have ensured all was done properly, and they likely would have onboarded the investor they were so hoping to win over.

Earlier, we reviewed the 6 most common incorporation errors. It's those errors that people often make when going the DIY route, and ultimately need to hire an attorney in order to fix the problems.

In addition, when incorporating, you've got to make important decisions regarding each of the following, and ensure each choice is right for your corporation:

1. Incorporate in the right jurisdiction (provincial or federal)
2. Name the corporation (ensuring no one else owns the rights to that name by performing a preliminary trademark search)
3. Properly define your share description
4. Properly define the corporation's activities
5. Complete and organize your corporate minute book (see next chapter)

This is the way I look at incorporation:

When you incorporate, you do so to set your business on solid legal footing and protect your interests and assets. Incorporation creates a separate business entity and offers you the benefit of limited liability to protect your personal assets and help secure your corporation's future.

Why would you take any risks with these important aspects of your life?

Usually there's only one reason: cash flow. So let me give

you some tips on how to incorporate properly, without breaking the bank.

3 Ways to Incorporate Right, on a Budget

1. DIY and Attorney Review

If you'd like to prepare your incorporation, get the forms completed and then have them reviewed by an attorney who understands your business and objectives.

Incorporating often does require a process of complicated agreements, so the advice of an attorney can be invaluable during the procedure. The attorney will be able to review your documents, make sure the right decisions are being made, and make recommendations to help you get started on the right legal footing. Once it's reviewed and approved, you can then submit everything to Corporations Canada or your provincial business registry.

An attorney can also offer assistance, suggestions and advice to help you raise capital from outside investors and lenders. He can address relevant tax and legal issues pertaining to the jurisdiction in which the business is incorporated and operated. If needed, an attorney can make the proper introductions for you to bankers, investors or accountants.

2. Online Incorporation

There are plenty of options for corporate services these days, from law firms to startups offering online incorporation packages and you have to find the best fit for you.

Because of the frequency with which I meet entrepreneurs who need help setting up and fixing up their corporations, we launched our online Incorporation Packages at Legal Logik. Just sign up online and our corporate team will complete or update your corporation, ensuring it's done correctly, and tailored to your needs and objectives.

As an entrepreneur myself, I know exactly what it's like to be starting a business and this is my way of helping other entrepreneurs like yourself set the stage for your future growth and successes.

As an entrepreneur, my mission is to help people turn their entrepreneurial dreams into a reality. I want to be there when their idea is just a dream and watch it materialize. That's the greatest part of my job.

3. Packaged Deal

More and more law firms are offering packaged deals whereby, through bundling, you get a much better price on the legal services you need to start up.

Since new businesses often need many of the same services, such as incorporation, contracts, a preliminary trademark search, and several hours of consultation, we launched Legal Logik's Start-Up Kit.

Notes:

CHAPTER EIGHT: Do You Need A Corporate Minute Book?

4 Practical Reasons Why You Need Minute Book

SUMMARY

1. Avoid Penalties

2. Secure Funding

3. Handle An Audit with Greater Ease

4. Sell Your Business

"The Minute Book is the DNA of the Corporation"

I often see a look of bewilderment in business owners' faces when I ask them if their minute book is up to date. The answers I usually get are a variation of one of the following:

a. What the hell is a minute book?
b. I think I or my accountant/lawyer/partner created one years ago.
c. Oh yes, I heard about that, and I don't need one.

Minute books are nothing more than the guts of the corporation or the DNA, serving as a register for the history of the corporation since its creation.

In this book, you will find everything from the by-laws governing how things work internally to the resolutions allowing the directors to make certain decisions for the corporation. You will also find the necessary approvals from the shareholders to make decisions, the registers of directors, shareholders and officers, and of course, the share certificate, which is like a receipt for the number of shares of the corporation a shareholder owns.

Minute books are also easy to recognize, since they are typically larger, thicker binders with a gold plaque with the corporate name etched on the front.

In reality, these books are created by either yourself or your lawyer, and then put on a shelf to collect dust until the next important decision is needed to be made. It could be resolutions by the board and shareholders, or signing on an anniversary date when it's time to re-elect the directors and confirm the financial statements of the corporation.

Much like your doctor's office, law firms usually have a room where these books are brimming from wall to wall, floor to ceiling, and kept in trust until consultation by you, your accountant, bankers, or in the event of a sale when the book is relied upon during due diligence.

Let's take control of our corporate documents once and for all and demystify what the minute book is all about and how it's an important piece of hardware that should be part of any healthy corporate strategy.

Most entrepreneurs know that when it comes time to incorporate, they can take the DIY route. They can use the Corporations Canada website and complete a federal incorporation or use the website of the *Registraire des Entreprises du Québec* (REQ) for a provincial incorporation. Doing it this way is attractive because it keeps costs down.

Why hire a lawyer to incorporate your business when you can do it on your own?

Well, there is a reason, and ignorance of it could be costly to you and your business' future.

When you take the DIY route, the government provides you with your certificate of incorporation, but doesn't supply any of the corporate documents you are required *by law*, nor a corporate minute book to organize these documents. Let's take a look at what the law says about the corporate minute book and why it's important to have one.

Your Corporate Minute Book: What the Law Says

A minute book can be described as the tool corporations use to organize and document their key corporate records. It holds the corporation's by-laws, organizational resolutions, share descriptions, registers and share certificates. Whether you incorporate provincially or federally, you need to have these documents.

Quebec Corporations

In Quebec, the *Loi sur les sociétés par actions* du Québec (LSAQ) outlines certain rules regulating provincial corporations. It provides that:

"A corporation must prepare and maintain, at its head office, records containing:

1. *The articles and the bylaws, and any unanimous shareholder agreement;*
2. *Minutes of meetings and resolutions of shareholders;*

3. *The names and domiciles of the directors, and the dates of the beginning and end of their term of office; and*

4. *A securities register."*

Federal Corporations

When you're incorporated federally, it's the CBCA (*Canada Business Corporations Act*) that sets forth the laws regarding your corporation. What the CBCA states is quite similar to that which is outlined in the LSAQ. Article 20 of the CBCA provides that:

"*A corporation shall prepare and maintain, at its registered office or at any other place in Canada designated by the directors, records containing...*"

And subsequently lists the following documents, among others:

- The articles and the by-laws and all the amendments thereto, and a copy of any unanimous shareholder agreement.
- Minutes of meetings and resolutions of shareholders.
- A securities register.

The laws for provincial and federal corporations are essentially the same, with one simple difference: A corporation incorporated federally can keep its minute book anywhere in Canada the directors choose, whereas a Quebec corporation must store theirs at their registered office within the province.

What this means is that if you incorporate your business, You need all the above corporate documents organized in a minute book (and that minute book needs to be kept up-to-date year to year).

4 Practical Reasons Why You Need A Minute Book

The above might leave you thinking that once you dish

out some cash for a corporate minute book, it can simply gather dust on a shelf. But besides the laws outlined in the LSAQ and the CBCA, there are actually practical business reasons to have an up-to-date corporate minute book.

Here are the 4 practical reasons you need a corporate minute book:

1. Avoid Penalties

Although rare, if you do not maintain a minute book, you can face statutory offences in the form of a fine.

2. Secure Funding

If you want to raise capital or secure a loan, third parties such as bankers, investors or accountants may want to review your corporate minute book as a way to evaluate the robustness of your business.

3. Handle An Audit with Greater Ease

If federal or provincial tax authorities choose to audit you, they may require access to your corporate minute book to evaluate your business structure. An up-to-date corporate minute book can help streamline the entire process, allowing the Canada Revenue Agency ("CRA") or other fiscal authorities to clarify issues and solve discrepancies.

4. Sell Your Business

If you're looking to sell your corporation at some point in the future, you'll want a professionally compiled and up-to-date corporate minute book.

To perform due diligence and evaluate your corporation, the buyer will want access to your corporate minute book. If it's out-of-date, incomplete, or non-existent, it might cost you the sale!

So do you need a corporate minute book? The answer is yes!

Notes:

CHAPTER NINE: Incorporated? Here Are the 4 Yearly Legal Obligations You Must Fulfill

SUMMARY

1. File Annual Declarations with the Respective Registry

2. Pay Annual Declaration Fees

3. Prepare Annual Resolutions

4. File Your Corporate Tax Return

© *Legal Logik, used under license*

> ## "Like a medical checkup, your incorporation needs attention at least once a year"

Incorporating your business is fairly simple, especially when you hire a law firm to do it for you. You submit your info and presto, you've got your certificate of incorporation!

Also don't forget the corporate minute book with all the required corporate documents, as required both by provincial and federal law. In addition to a minute book, once incorporated, there are a few other obligations you must fulfill each year.

Having worked with thousands of entrepreneurs and startups, there is one thing I see all too frequently:

An entrepreneur incorporates his business and the next thing he knows, a year or two has gone by. He hasn't filed the annual declarations, paid the annual government fees, or completed the other yearly obligations that must be fulfilled, such as preparation of annual resolutions. Those to-dos, deadlines and paperwork just fell by the wayside as he focused on what was really important: building his business!

Clients like this come to us to solve this problem. Having submitted documents late or not at all, there is lots to catch up on, and the government has slapped the corporation with penalties.

Sometimes, the government - provincial or federal - has actually dissolved their corporation. We are called upon to correct these errors. We get the paperwork up to date, ensure fees and penalties are paid, and, if the corporation has been dissolved, we will work to get it revived. When this happens, we are happy to take over and fix this for clients, but we much prefer helping them keep their corporation in good legal standing from the beginning, to avoid fines and additional fees.

If you're incorporated, you need to know about the annual corporate requirements to stay in the game.

Incorporated? Here are Your 4 Yearly Corporate Obligations

1. **File Annual Declarations with the Respective Registry**

   If you incorporated provincially, you must complete and file an annual declaration with the *Registraire des Entreprises du Québec (REQ)*.

   If you registered federally, you must file your annual declaration with Corporations Canada as well as the *REQ*. This must be done each year even if your corporate information remains unchanged.

2. **Pay Annual Declaration Fees**

   If you incorporated your business federally, you must pay the annual declaration fee each year.

3. **Prepare Annual Resolutions**

   Each year, annual resolutions must be prepared for your corporate minute book, updating your corporate ledgers and by-laws, documenting any changes in your corporation, and approving your corporation's financial statements in accordance with its fiscal year-end date.

4. File Your Corporate/Sales Tax Return(s)

Even if your corporation earns no revenue, you must file a corporate tax return with both the provincial and federal governments.

What If You Don't Fulfill These Obligations?

Watch out! If you don't fulfill each of these obligations, and fulfill them on time, there are consequences.

Both the provincial and federal governments may impose fines, or worse, dissolve your corporation.

Quebec Incorporation

1. If your annual declarations are not filed within six months of the corporation's anniversary, the Québec government may impose a penalty.

2. If not filed for two consecutive years, the Quebec government may dissolve your business from the Quebec Enterprise Register (REQ).

3. If dissolved, it is possible to revive your corporation. To revive a Quebec corporation, you must complete a *Demande de révocation de radiation* and pay a filing fee, in addition to any legal fees. You will also have to file any outstanding declarations and pay any unpaid fees from previous years.

Federal Incorporation

1. If your annual declarations are not filed for two consecutive years, the federal government may dissolve your corporation.

2. If dissolved, it is possible to revive a federal corporation. To revive a federal corporation, you will need to complete and sign Form 15 – Articles of Revival, complete a NUANS name search to verify that the corporate name you were

incorporated under is still available, and pay a filing fee, in addition to any legal fees.

Your Corporate Tax Return

I asked Tax Lawyer Joseph Jalkh, *L.L.M Fisc.* to explain the deadlines and rules around filing corporate tax returns:

Corporations must generally file, within 6 months after their year-end, their corporate income tax returns. However, tax installments may be due on a monthly or trimestrial basis (except during its first year of creation) depending on factors such as their revenue of last year and status (Canadian-controlled private corporation). Failure to file could result in a penalty of up to 5% of the unpaid amount from the CRA plus 1% of this unpaid tax for each complete month that the return is late, up to a maximum of 12 months.

It is to be noted that Revenue Quebec applies similar provisions so you can end up getting interest and penalties from both jurisdictions!

Also, if you're registered for sales tax (GST/QST), you must file a sales tax return on a monthly, trimestrial or annual basis depending on the choice you have made upon registration, or the amount of your sales for your past fiscal year.

An easy option to ensure your corporate obligations are fulfilled, and your corporation remains in good legal standing at all times, is to find a legal or corporate services firm offering a Annual Corporate Maintenance service. You can put your corporate obligations on autopilot, ensuring everything is done right, on time, every year. Because clients of ours were falling behind with their annual maintenance, we created just such a service to save them from the hassles and headaches.

Notes:

Notes:

CHAPTER TEN: Do You Need A Shareholders' Agreement?

SUMMARY

The Shareholders' Agreement specifies what happens if a shareholder:

1. Does not fulfill his responsibilities and commitments

2. Wishes to leave the corporation

3. Commits fraud

4. Is negligent

5. Wants to sell his shares

6. Goes bankrupt

7. Passes away

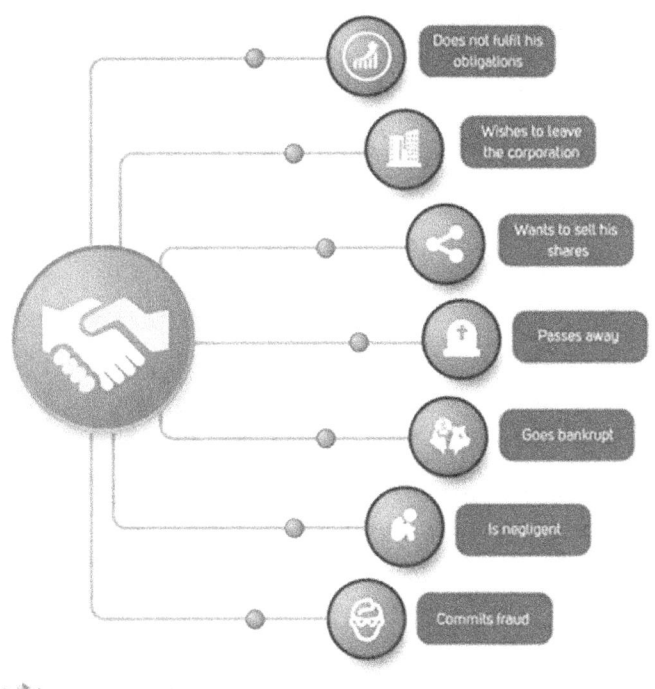

THE 7 PILLARS OF A SHAREHOLDERS'
AGREEMENT

The law is silent on a number of situations that can impact the corporation. A shareholders' agreement aims to fill the gaps, specifying what will happen if a director or shareholder...

- Does not fulfil his obligations
- Wishes to leave the corporation
- Wants to sell his shares
- Passes away
- Goes bankrupt
- Is negligent
- Commits fraud

LEGALLOGIK

> *"A Shareholders Agreement is as important to the corporation as the Canadian Constitution is to Canadian citizens"*

Incorporating your business is a momentous step. Maybe you're launching a new venture with your sights set high, or your existing business has grown and you're ready to enjoy the benefits of incorporation. And while you have great hopes for the future, you never know what can happen when you have partners.

Consider the experience of a corporation I recently worked with. Two business partners teamed up and incorporated their business and were now the two proud shareholders in a new corporation. Things started off swimmingly with each partner respecting his end of the bargain, fulfilling the roles and responsibilities he committed himself to delivering for the corporation.

A few months into their respective roles, one of the two shareholders unexpectedly died, leaving the surviving shareholder alone to run the business with the deceased shareholder's brother and liquidator (a.k.a. executor of his estate), Max Prawfit, who had completely different plans for the business.

From the moment Max Prawfit came into the business, he tried to call the shots. He fired people, took control of all finances, and began preparations to make the business appear healthier than it actually was in order to sell it on the market. The surviving shareholder disagreed, and the two of them fought incessantly about everything from the operations of the business to ordering soap for the bathroom.

To make matters worse, the majority of the staff called an emergency meeting with the surviving shareholder, giving him an ultimatum: Max Prawfit was impossible to work for and was so condescending to them that if he didn't leave, they all would.

What could the surviving shareholder do? How could he let this man continue to ruin the business that had taken 30 years to build?

Had the founding shareholders completed the exercise of negotiating and signing a shareholders' agreement, they could have considered a clause specifically stating what would happen in the event one of the shareholders passes away. The steps to take for the corporation in such a situation would have been clear, and the case would have been easier to resolve.

Unfortunately, the founding shareholders never signed a shareholders' agreement. The result was that, even though one of the shareholders had passed away, his estate, administered by Max Prawfit, still had rights to the value of the corporation, and was able to control the deceased shareholder's shares, with all decision-making authority related to those shares.

Even without the active participation of a rogue executor like Max Prawfit, if the surviving shareholder were to continue operating the business himself, and make it a smashing success, he still might find himself facing a legal battle for rights to the corporation's assets from his former partner's heirs. This could result in years of litigation and a small fortune in legal fees, which could keep an army of lawyers busy for years.

Keeping Your Corporation Out of the Legal Grey Zone

There is a long list of occurrences that may negatively impact your corporation, and you may not be prepared for any of them.

Directors are mandated to oversee the affairs of the corporation and report back to the shareholders that own the corporation. Any one of the seven following events, can change the course of the business, if a director or shareholder:

1. **Does not fulfill their responsibilities and commitments**

   Imagine you expect that your fellow shareholder, who has a degree in finance, will take care of all finances related to the operations of the business. Your partner, however, is not interested in finance and prefers the operational side of the business. To avoid misunderstandings, each partners responsibilities should be clarified.

2. **Wishes to leave the corporation**

People change, regardless of whether or not the corporation is doing well. If a shareholder leaves the country and abandons his role within the corporation in order to fulfill another lifelong dream, it should be made clear what would happen with their shares to avoid paralyzing the corporation.

3. **Commits fraud**

You had no idea that your fellow shareholder also had a gambling problem? If he steals money from the corporation to fuel his addiction, there should be consequences for him to continue owning those shares in order to protect the corporation, such as forcing him to forfeit his shares at a discount.

4. **Is negligent**

Does your fellow shareholder seem to have better things to do besides overseeing the operations of the corporation? He shows up late every day, even trades on the stock market when he should be overseeing the quality control of production in the plant.

One of the orders that ships right under his nose is blatantly defective and could have easily been discovered with the simplest of oversight. Now the customer wants a complete reimbursement and damages for stocking and selling a defective product.

A negligent shareholder can be sanctioned and reprimanded for his behaviour.

5. **Wants to sell his shares to family members or business partners**

The founding shareholders of a corporation don't go into business together thinking about who in each other's circle of friends and family they will be forced to deal with, in the event that shareholder wants out.

There could be language used to bind the shareholders to first offer their shares to one another in priority to any third party.

It can also be agreed between the parties that in the event that either of them receive an offer from a third party, that it first be presented to the other shareholder, who, in turn, also has the first option to buy out the shareholder upon similar conditions.

6. Goes bankrupt

This can happen for any number of reasons, and the last thing the corporation needs is for the appointed licensed insolvency trustee orthe creditors meddling in the affairs of the corporation by asserting control or rights to the bankrupted shareholders' shares.

7. Passes away

The story of Max Prawfit highlights what can happen in the event of the death of a shareholder.

Various mechanisms can be drafted and agreed upon to avoid this deadlock situation, such as forcing the deceased shareholder's estate to sell the shares to the surviving shareholder at market price.

The law is actually silent on these matters, and if they occur, you, your corporation, and its directors and shareholders are left in a legal grey zone. As a result, any of these events, amongst others, could lead to disputes or legal battles, which could take months, even years, to resolve.

That's why a shareholders' agreement is absolutely crucial when you incorporate. A professionally drafted shareholder agreement is the best way to avoid future headaches. It helps protect you against the consequences of unplanned events, and their impacts on shareholders, by setting down in writing what actions would be taken in any unforeseen circumstances.

When unexpected events occur, many entrepreneurs have been saved by the terms of their shareholders' agreement, signed at the outset of their business relationship.

Finally, a shareholders' agreement can help on post-mortem tax planning by including specific stipulations on the purchase or transfer of the shares of the deceased shareholder to limit his tax liability upon death.

Getting Your Shareholders' Agreement Right

Like sitting down with your religious leader before getting married, a shareholders' agreement forces the partners to embark on an exercise to consider important business decisions, to learn more about one another, and set realistic expectations from the outset.

The exercise provides clear terms and answers to important business considerations, such as:

1. **What will the obligations of each of the shareholders be?**

   Defining key roles such as who will be in charge of sales, operations, finances etc. are important to clearly map out responsibilities within the business.

   It's true that startup founders tend to do everything and anything that needs to be done, from mopping the floors to driving around the city delivering orders. I always recommend, however, that the partners provide general guidelines around what each will do and what each will bring to the table, without it being so detailed that the language narrows the scope of each partner's role.

2. **What will happen if the corporation needs additional funding?**

This is so often overlooked when starting a business, and failing to consider it can lead to the business having difficulties if it becomes cash-poor.

Shareholders can decide how to raise cash when the corporation is in need and even set orders of priority. They can have the corporation apply for a bank loan, lend the money themselves in the proportion of their shares at a predetermined interest rate, even sell equity as needed. There's no right order, the importance of the exercise is to think about how to act during a cash crunch.

3. **What will happen in the event that one of the shareholders passes away?**

The story of Max Prawfit exemplifies how important it is to provide for the death of a shareholder.

Besides the option to provide that the estate of the deceased shareholder sell his shares back to the corporation, having the proper insurance policy is part of any succession strategy to ensure that the corporation has the cash on hand to pay for the shares.

Working with an experienced insurance broker can unlock great opportunities for the corporation and shareholders. Key-man insurance, for instance, can compensate the corporation in the event of the death of a "key" shareholder who was a driving-force behind the business.

Insurance is also part of a common tax planning strategy, whereby the corporation can subscribe to the policy and, in certain cases, actually deduct a part of the premiums. Make sure to consult your insurance broker when drafting your shareholders' agreement.

4. **What rules will be set down regarding the approval and/or signing of contracts or paying expenses?**

Some shareholders want to make sure more than one shareholder signs off on important decisions.

I often see situations where shareholders will require there to be at least two authorized signatories for contract approval (example, with a new suppliers), or signing cheques in excess of a certain amount (example, $10,000 and over). This forces the shareholders to consult one another for important financial decisions, without bogging down the corporation with smaller decisions.

5. **In what circumstances will a shareholder be able to leave the corporation?**

For startups, ensuring that indecisive or less committed shareholders do not affect the stability of the corporation is crucial.

In the early years of a startup, the corporate culture is taking shape, customers are eventually coming around and trying your product or service, and every dollar counts.

For these and other reasons we can stipulate that a shareholder must remain in the corporation for a certain period, say by way of a moratorium for 2 years, during which time they cannot sell their shares, invoke a shotgun clause (the nuclear style clause that provokes the end of the relationship) or pose any other action that would detract the corporation from their regular business activities.

6. **How will decisions be made and how will voting rights work (2 out of 3, unanimous, etc.)?**

Although a corporation may have three equal shareholders, we can provide that certain decisions that are considered essential be made unanimously. Similarly, we can also provide that any one of the three can make a specific decision without consulting the others, or even require the consent of two thirds of the shareholders.

7. **What rules shall be set in place preventing directors and shareholders from conflicts of interest?**

It's not uncommon for my clients to operate multiple businesses, often with different business partners, in the same industry. That's perfectly fine, as long as all of the shareholders agree to and understand that one of their partners will have multiple interests in potentially competing businesses.

That may be reasonable if, for example, you're a restaurant entrepreneur who runs a steakhouse concept with one group of shareholders, and a vegan concept with another group of shareholders, as the two will never seemingly compete with one another.

It may be more concerning however, if the entrepreneur shareholder is part of two separate corporations, and also happens to be a world renowned scientist with a patented drug to treat a very rare strain of influenza.

In the case of the scientist, because of the niche industry and expertise, he would want his fellow shareholders to ensure that they do not compete with him directly or indirectly, and put themselves in a situation of conflict of interest that would undermine his role as a shareholder.

Notes:

Conclusion

Law is dynamic. It's an incredible social tradition that's been passed down from previous generations and provides order and stability in our daily lives.

The corporation is the golden example of legal creativity, design and execution. It exists purely from our imagination, allowing us to organize our businesses to protect ourselves, to raise capital, and to ensure a legacy.

The centuries-old tradition of incorporation will continue to be a dominant form of business organization for as long as we collectively trust that it provides the benefits we expect of it.

Once reserved for large national businesses that had the political and financial clout to make use of its benefits, corporations are now available to every entrepreneur with a dream, and it has become my mission to emphasize its usefulness and power.

Your legacy starts today. Choosing the right legal vehicle to drive your dreams into the fast lane, while ensuring you are protected along the way, will clear the road towards financial success.